ENGINEERING

YOU CAN EAT

MEGAN BORGERT-SPANIOL

Consulting Editor, Diane Craig, MA/Reading Specialist

Super Sandcastle

An Imprint of Abdo Publishing
abdobooks.com

ABDOBOOKS.COM

Published by Abdo Publishing, a division of ABDO, PO Box 398166, Minneapolis, Minnesota 55439. Copyright © 2019 by Abdo Consulting Group, Inc. International copyrights reserved in all countries. No part of this book may be reproduced in any form without written permission from the publisher. Super SandCastle™ is a trademark and logo of Abdo Publishing.

Printed in the United States of America, North Mankato, Minnesota
102018
012019

Design: Emily O'Malley, Mighty Media, Inc.
Production: Mighty Media, Inc.
Editor: Liz Salzmann
Cover Photographs: Mighty Media, Inc.; Shutterstock
Interior Photographs: Mighty Media, Inc.; Shutterstock

The following manufacturers/names appearing in this book are trademarks: Essential Everyday®, Glico® Pocky®, Little Debbie®, Nutella®, Pillsbury Creamy Supreme®, Target®, Voortman™

Library of Congress Control Number: 2018948859

Publisher's Cataloging-in-Publication Data
Names: Borgert-Spaniol, Megan, author.
Title: Engineering you can eat / by Megan Borgert-Spaniol.
Description: Minneapolis, Minnesota : Abdo Publishing, 2019 | Series: Super simple science you can snack on
Identifiers: ISBN 9781532117244 (lib. bdg.) | ISBN 9781532170102 (ebook)
Subjects: LCSH: Engineering--Juvenile literature. | Cooking--Juvenile literature. | Science--Experiments--Juvenile literature. | Gastronomy--Juvenile literature.
Classification: DDC 641.0--dc23

Super SandCastle™ books are created by a team of professional educators, reading specialists, and content developers around five essential components—phonemic awareness, phonics, vocabulary, text comprehension, and fluency—to assist young readers as they develop reading skills and strategies and increase their general knowledge. All books are written, reviewed, and leveled for guided reading and early reading intervention programs for use in shared, guided, and independent reading and writing activities to support a balanced approach to literacy instruction.

TO ADULT HELPERS

The projects in this book are fun and simple. There are just a few things to remember to keep kids safe. Some projects require the use of sharp objects. Also, kids may be using messy ingredients. Make sure they protect their clothes and work surfaces. Review the projects before starting, and be ready to assist when necessary.

KEY SYMBOL

Watch for this warning symbol in this book. Here is what it means.

SHARP!
You will be working with something sharp. Get help!

CONTENTS

WHAT IS ENGINEERING?

Engineering is the application of science and math to solve practical problems. People who **design** and build things to solve **specific** problems are called engineers.

The oldest form of engineering is the designing and building of structures. These structures include roads, bridges, buildings, tunnels, and more.

THE ROMANS BUILT SOME OF THE FIRST BRIDGES MORE THAN 1,500 YEARS AGO.

ANCIENT PYRAMIDS

In ancient times, some civilizations built **pyramids** to honor gods and royalty. Most of these structures were made of stone and took years to build. Many still stand today. Some of the most well-known pyramids are located in Egypt.

THE PYRAMIDS OF GIZA IN EGYPT WERE BUILT MORE THAN 4,000 YEARS AGO.

ENGINEERING TODAY

Today, there are many types of engineering. These include computer engineering, chemical engineering, and electrical engineering.

But engineers also still **design** and build structures. This field is called civil engineering. Many of the most well-known engineering marvels were built by civil engineers.

BURJ KHALIFA IN UNITED ARAB EMIRATES IS THE TALLEST BUILDING IN THE WORLD.

THE CHANNEL TUNNEL IS 31 MILES (50 KM) LONG.

THE BEIJING NATIONAL STADIUM CAN HOLD 91,000 PEOPLE.

CHANNEL TUNNEL

The Channel Tunnel is an underwater rail tunnel. It opened in 1994. The tunnel runs under the English Channel, connecting England and France.

BEIJING NATIONAL STADIUM

The Beijing National **Stadium** in China was built for the 2008 Summer Olympic Games. The stadium is also called the "Bird's Nest" for its shape and **interlocking** steel pieces. It is one of the world's largest steel structures.

ENGINEERING SNACKS

You can learn a lot about engineering by making the fun snacks in this book!

GET READY

* Ask an adult for **permission** to use kitchen tools and ingredients.

* Read the snack's list of tools and ingredients. Make sure you have everything you need.

* Does a snack require ingredients you don't like? Get creative! Find other ingredients you enjoy instead.

SNACK CLEAN & SAFE

* Clean your work surface before you start.

* Wash your hands before you work with food.

* Keep your work area tidy. This makes it easier to find what you need.

* Ask an adult for help when handling sharp or hot objects.

CLEANING UP

* Don't waste unused ingredients! Store leftover ingredients to use later.

* Clean your work surface. Wash any dishes or tools you used.

* Wash your hands before you eat your snack!

INGREDIENTS & TOOLS

APPLE

CHOCOLATE FROSTING

CHOCOLATE POCKY STICKS

FRUIT LEATHER

GRAHAM CRACKERS

HONEY GRAHAM CEREAL

MINI MARSHMALLOWS

NUTELLA

PEANUT BUTTER

SHREDDED COCONUT

SMALL POWDERED DOUGHNUTS

TWIZZLERS PULL 'N' PEEL CANDY

VANILLA FROSTING

VANILLA SNACK CAKES

VANILLA WAFER COOKIES

HERE ARE SOME OF THE INGREDIENTS AND TOOLS YOU WILL NEED TO MAKE THE SNACKS IN THIS BOOK.

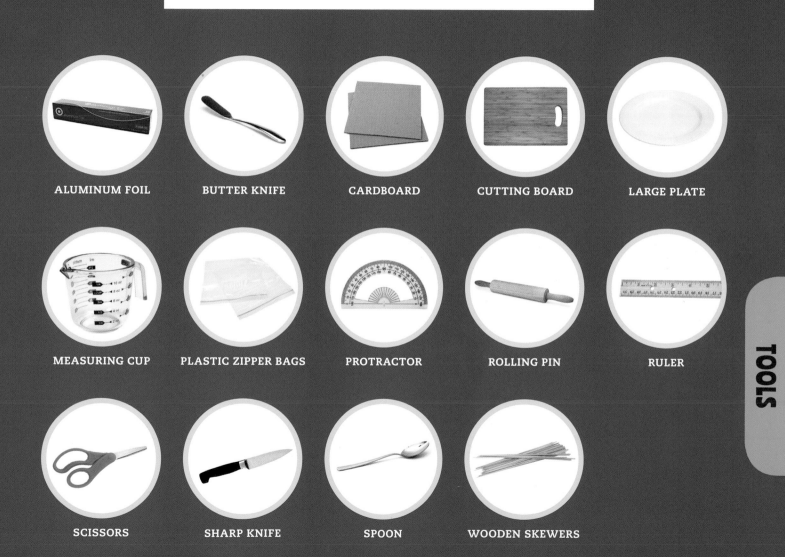

ALUMINUM FOIL

BUTTER KNIFE

CARDBOARD

CUTTING BOARD

LARGE PLATE

MEASURING CUP

PLASTIC ZIPPER BAGS

PROTRACTOR

ROLLING PIN

RULER

SCISSORS

SHARP KNIFE

SPOON

WOODEN SKEWERS

TOOLS

DELICIOUS EGYPTIAN PYRAMIDS

INGREDIENTS

- frosting
- honey graham cereal
- graham crackers

TOOLS

- spoon
- measuring cup
- 2 plastic zipper bags
- scissors
- large plate
- rolling pin

The Egyptian **pyramids** are considered marvels of the ancient world. They were built with millions of stone blocks. Try building your own pyramid with crunchy cereal squares!

1. Seal ¼ cup of frosting in a plastic bag. Cut one corner of the bag to make a small hole.

2. Gently **squeeze** the bag until frosting comes out of the hole. Use it to draw a square on the plate. Put more frosting inside the square.

3. Place cereal squares over the frosting in rows. This is the base of the pyramid.

4. Put more frosting on top of the cereal. Add another layer of cereal.

5. Repeat step 4 to add more layers of cereal. Make each layer slightly smaller than the layer below it. Top the pyramid with half of a cereal square.

6. Seal three graham crackers in the other plastic bag. Roll a rolling pin over the bag to crush the crackers into **crumbs**.

7. Use the graham cracker crumbs to create a sandy desert around your pyramid.

APPLE IGLOO ⊘

INGREDIENTS
- apple
- peanut butter or Nutella
- mini marshmallows
- shredded coconut (optional)

TOOLS
- cutting board
- sharp knife
- large plate
- butter knife

The Inuit people live in the Arctic. They build igloos with blocks of snow. An igloo traps the body heat of those inside it. This is how people stay warm. Try building your own igloo out of food!

1. Ask an adult to help you cut the core out of the apple. Then cut the apple in half vertically.

2. Place one half of the apple cut-side down on the cutting board. Cut a small arch into one end of the apple. This is the igloo's entrance.

3. Move the apple to the plate. Spread a thin layer of peanut butter or Nutella over the apple.

4. Press marshmallows onto the peanut butter around the entrance arch.

Continued on the next page.

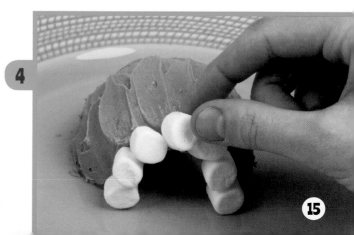

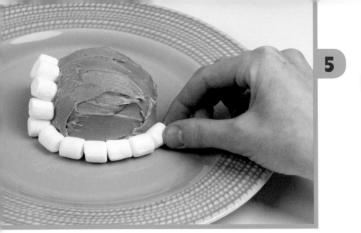

5

6

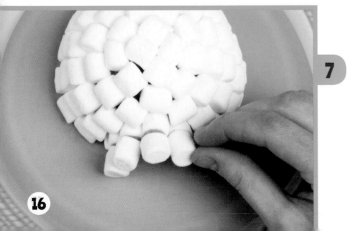

7

5. Cover the rest of the apple with marshmallows. Start by placing the marshmallows in a line along the bottom edge of the apple.

6. Continue placing marshmallows in rows around the apple until the apple is covered.

7. Use peanut butter or Nutella to add a second layer of marshmallows around the entrance arch.

8. Try using shredded coconut to create a snowy scene around the igloo!

SCIENCE BITE

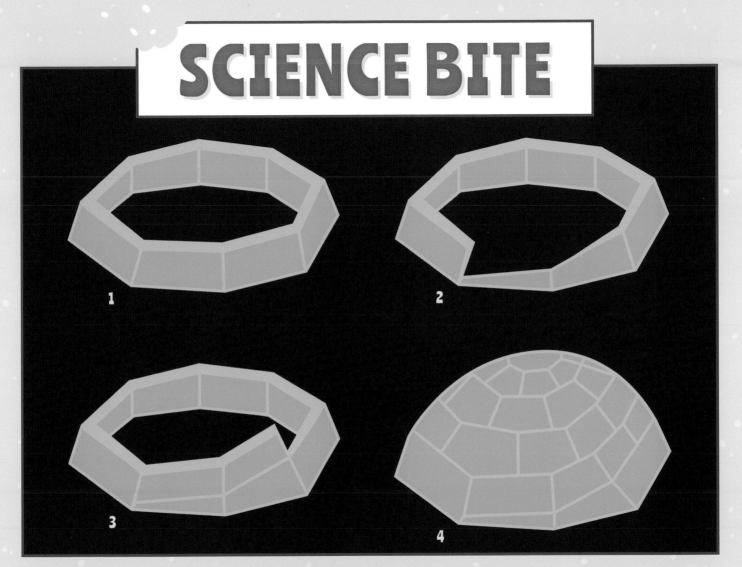

1

2

3

4

THE BLOCKS USED TO BUILD IGLOOS ARE USUALLY 2 FEET (61 CM) TALL AND 4 FEET (122 CM) WIDE. THEY ARE 8 INCHES (20 CM) THICK. THE BLOCKS IN THE FIRST LAYER ARE CUT TO FORM A SLOPE. THIS CREATES A SPIRAL WHEN THE OTHER LAYERS ARE ADDED.

TASTY TEPEE

INGREDIENTS

- Twizzlers Pull 'n' Peel candy
- chocolate frosting
- chocolate Pocky sticks
- fruit leather

TOOLS

- spoon
- measuring cup
- plastic zipper bag
- scissors
- large plate

North American Plains Indians build structures called tepees. A tepee has long poles wrapped in animal skins. It is easy to take down and move to a new location. Build your own sweet tepee!

1. Pull a candy rope off of a Twizzler. Set the rope within easy reach. Eat the rest of the Twizzler!

2. Seal ¼ cup of frosting in the plastic bag. Cut one corner of the bag to make a small hole.

3. Gently **squeeze** the bag until frosting comes out of the hole. Use it to make six dots in a circle on the plate.

Continued on the next page.

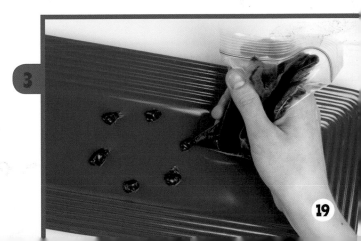

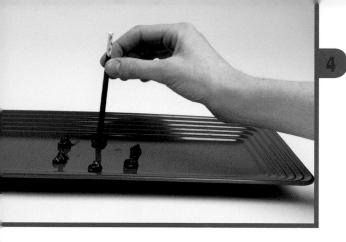

4. Place the chocolate-coated end of a Pocky stick in one of the dots of frosting. Let the stick lean toward the center of the circle. Hold the top of the stick with one hand.

5. With your other hand, place another Pocky stick into another dot of frosting. Let it lean in toward the center of the plate. Hold the tops of both sticks together.

6. Repeat step 5 until a Pocky stick has been placed in each dot of frosting. Hold the tops of the sticks together in a bunch.

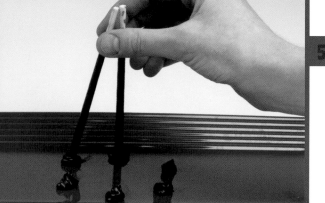

7. Carefully wrap the candy rope around the sticks to hold them together. You can ask an adult or a friend to help you do this.

8. Gently **squeeze** frosting along the length of each stick.

9. Cut pieces of fruit leather into triangles that fit over the spaces between the sticks.

10. Press the fruit leather against the frosting on the sticks. Leave one space uncovered. This is the door into the tepee.

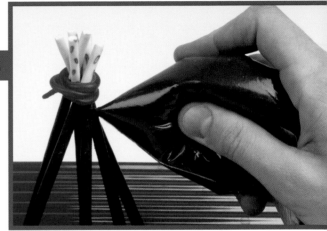

LEANING TOWER OF PASTRIES

INGREDIENTS

- 2 vanilla snack cakes
- 6 small powdered doughnuts
- chocolate frosting

TOOLS

- cardboard
- ruler
- scissors
- aluminum foil
- wooden skewer
- protractor (optional)
- cutting board
- sharp knife
- spoon
- measuring cup
- plastic zipper bag

Italy's Leaning Tower of Pisa is a bell tower famous for its **tilt**. Engineers have worked to straighten it. But the tower is still tilted today. You can construct your own leaning tower out of doughnuts!

1. Cut five squares out of cardboard. Make each one 5 by 5 inches (13 × 13 cm). Pile the squares on top of one another. Wrap aluminum foil around the pile. This is your tower's base.

2. Stick the pointed end of the skewer into the center of the base at a slight angle. Instead of making a 90-**degree** angle with the base, it should make about an 86-degree angle. You can use a protractor to help set this angle.

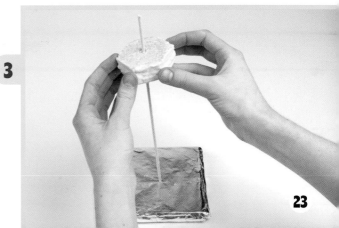

3. Hold a snack cake centered over the skewer. Gently press the cake onto the skewer. Slide the cake down until it rests on the base.

Continued on the next page.

4. Cut one or two small pieces of cardboard. Slip them under the snack cake to help support its **tilt**.

5. Slide a doughnut over the skewer until it rests on the cake.

6. Repeat step 5 until there are six doughnuts on top of the cake.

7. Have an adult help you cut the sides off a snack cake to make it smaller.

8. Slide the small cake onto the skewer to rest on the top doughnut.

9. Cut off any part of the skewer that sticks up above the tower.

10. Seal ¼ cup of frosting in the plastic bag. Cut one corner of the bag to make a small hole.

11. Gently **squeeze** the bag until frosting comes out of the hole. Use it to draw arches around each level of the tower.

EDIBLE EIFFEL TOWER

INGREDIENTS

- vanilla frosting
- vanilla wafer cookies

TOOLS

- spoon
- measuring cup
- plastic zipper bag
- scissors
- large plate
- cutting board
- sharp knife

The Eiffel Tower was constructed for the 1889 World's Fair in Paris, France. For 40 years, it was the world's tallest structure. Engineer an **edible** Eiffel Tower using only two materials!

1. Seal ¼ cup of frosting in the plastic bag. Cut one corner of the bag to make a small hole.

2. Gently **squeeze** the bag until frosting comes out of the hole. Use it to draw four large dots of frosting on the plate. The dots should form a rectangle that is about the size of two wafer cookies set side by side.

3. Have an adult help you cut two wafer cookies in half.

4. Place one end of each cookie piece in one of the dots of frosting. Each cookie piece should lean slightly toward the center of the plate.

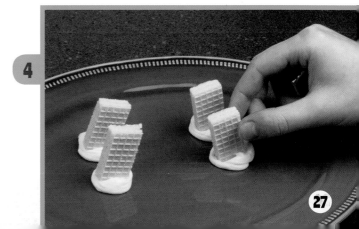

Continued on the next page.

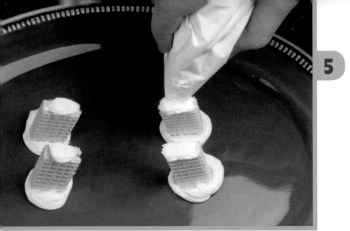

5

6

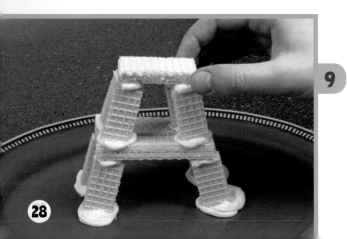

9

5. **Squeeze** a dot of frosting onto the top of each cookie piece.

6. Lay two whole wafer cookies next to each other on top of the four cookie pieces. This is the floor of the first level of the tower.

7. Squeeze a dot of frosting near each corner of the floor.

8. Repeat steps 3 and 4 to make supports for the second level of the tower.

9. Squeeze a dot of frosting onto the top of each support cookie. Cut a wafer cookie piece that fits on the supports. Place it on the supports to create the floor of the second level.

10. Cover the second floor with frosting.

11. Cut a piece of cookie that is slightly smaller than the second floor. Place it on top of the frosting.

12. Set two wafer cookies next to each other. Cut the left cookie from the top right corner to the bottom left corner. Cut the right cookie from the top left corner to the bottom right corner.

13. Put frosting between the middle cookie pieces. Press them together to form a triangle.

14. Use frosting to stick the triangle to the top of the tower.

15. Cut a small cookie square. Use frosting to stick it to the top of the tower.

CONCLUSION

Engineering is the use of science and math to solve practical problems. Engineers create exciting and useful products including computers, medicines, cars, **skyscrapers**, and more!

MAKING SNACKS IS JUST ONE WAY TO LEARN ABOUT ENGINEERING. HOW WILL YOU CONTINUE YOUR ENGINEERING ADVENTURE?

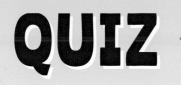

QUIZ

1. BUILDING STRUCTURES IS A NEW FORM OF ENGINEERING. TRUE OR FALSE?

2. THE CHANNEL TUNNEL GOES UNDER WHAT BODY OF WATER?

3. WHAT ARE IGLOOS MADE OUT OF?

LEARN MORE ABOUT IT!

YOU CAN FIND OUT MORE ABOUT ENGINEERING AT THE LIBRARY. OR YOU CAN ASK AN ADULT TO HELP YOU FIND INFORMATION ABOUT ENGINEERING ON THE INTERNET!

ANSWERS: 1. FALSE 2. THE ENGLISH CHANNEL 3. BLOCKS OF SNOW

GLOSSARY

crumb – a tiny piece of something, especially food.

degree – a unit used to measure the size of an angle.

design – to plan how something will appear or work.

edible – safe to eat.

interlocking – having parts that fit together and connect tightly.

permission – when a person in charge says it's okay to do something.

pyramid – a shape that has a square base and four triangular sides that form a point at the top.

skyscraper – a very tall building.

specific – about or related to a certain kind of thing.

spiral – a line that curves around a central point in sloping layers.

squeeze – to press the sides of something together.

stadium – a large building with an open area for sporting events surrounded by rows of seats.

tilt – to be positioned at a slope or an angle.